Leechcraft

David Ward

Leechcraft

Text copyright©2024 David Ward
Cover image: Elliot Ward

ISBN 978-1-7393239-5-0

British Library Cataloguing in Publication Data.
A catalogue record for this book is available from the British Library.

3 5 4 2

First Published in Great Britain
Hawkwood Books 2024
Blackpool Enterprise Centre FY4 1EW

Printed and bound in Great Britain by CPI Group (UK) Ltd.
Croydon CR0 4YY

For D.C.

"These poems are mesmerising. Written in simple, musical language, complete with repetition, refrain and rhyme, they dress the darkest matter in the lightest of clothing. These deeply felt, singing poems are *for* our times – but just as surely will have long lives."
KEVIN CROSSLEY-HOLLAND: *Gravity for Beginners*

"A concentrated, intense sequence. Two weeks on, these poems continue to haunt. The world they occupy draws the reader in, and once that reader comes to terms with that world and its flickering light, they have the strangest power, like images glimpsed out of chiaroscuro."
SEAN STREET: *Journey into Space*

"Like a message from lost Albion!"
TIM FREEMAN: *Background Noise*

"A dark and fascinating mythscape... *The Blunted Axe* is such a mysterious and mystical way of looking at the natural world."
NATALIE LINH BOLDERSTON: *The Protection of Ghosts*

"The poems sit lightly on the page, seeming like wraiths in the mist. But they are sharper than they seem, pinned to the page by acute observations."
FREDA DAVIS: *Write Out Loud*

"A world of haunting images, where characters explore feelings of loss, hope and beauty, against a backdrop of the inexorable passage of time. Each poem invites us to step into a story alive with sensory detail and evocative imagery."
TAMIKO DOOLEY: *Seasons of Love around the Rising Sun*

CONTENTS

The Crow was made of Twigs

The crow was made of twigs.

They killed it in the high wood
and hung its bones to dry.

It watched the furrowed fields
with their malice in its eye.

The crow was made of twigs.

Dark feathers stripped and shredded
so that it could never fly.

They broke its beak with clawhammers
to still its doleful cry.

The crow was made of twigs.

They nailed its heart to a bloodied tree
beneath the iron grey sky.

The Dark Hawk

They took the boy from his house
the day that the dark hawk came.

He told them he had seen it —
he said he'd seen it come.

They led him to the old oak tree
by the beating of a drum.

They lashed him to its branches
and left him hanging there,

pressed garlic tight inside his mouth,
tied larkspur in his hair.

'He said he'd seen the red fish
lie bloated in the stream.'

'He said he'd seen the white horse ride
as if it was a dream.'

They went back to his house
and nailed up the door.

They smashed in every window
so the hawk would come no more.

At night there came a girl
who cut him from the tree.

She pressed her body to him
and told him they were wrong.

She kissed him sweet and lonely
and sang a soothing song.

She brought him bread and water
but in the morning he was gone –
the boy who said he'd seen the hawk,
he said he'd seen it come.

They rattled pans and broken pails
up and down the lanes,

lit bonfires on the hilltop
and fanned the fearful flames,

but when they looked into the sky —
the hawk it came again.

She Walks the Lanes

She walks the lanes with a basket
    which she holds beneath her arm.

She gathers briars and gossamer
    to weave a cunning charm

from the foxes in the long dark fields
    who mean to do her harm.

    In the dead night, by candlelight,
    she twists her threads around.
    In the dead night, by candlelight,
    she works without a sound.

But down the lane comes shuffling
    a boy who has no tongue.
Down the lane comes shuffling
    a boy with a skylark's song.

He knocks upon her window
    and she turns ashen pale,
as there upon her cottage door
    he nails a fox's tail.

Oh, the hares they run in the meadow
and blackbirds sing sweet down the lane,
but the basket lies by her stone-cold hearth
and will never be filled again.

Down by the Byre

She went out to find him, into the night
    though she could not know he was there.

Her head was filled with the moonlight
    as she waited down by the byre.

She heard his footsteps come slowly,
    then she smelt the breath of his pain.

He said he'd been out by the high wood,
    his jacket was drenched with the rain.

She asked why his hands were shaking —
    He said, 'For want of your touch.'

He said his body was aching
    all for the lack of her love.

She wrapped her arms around him
    to take the chill fever away —

But up in the dark, in the high wood,
    the miller's young daughter lay.

The Lych-Gate

Outside by the lych-gate, an orphan wind is stealing.
Outside by the lych-gate,
    a switch-eyed woman kneeling.

She holds a broken cup
    in her crooked hand.
She lifts it to her lips
    then casts it to the ground.

Outside by the lych-gate, the tall trees all a-shiver.
The woman asks for blessing,
    but no-one will forgive her.

She pulls a cowl about her head
    and curses out the weather.
She says she came here all alone
    but we must leave together.

Outside by the lych-gate
    one grey horse stands waiting.
Outside by the lych-gate,
    lies the road no-one has taken.

The Burning

Black smoke from the back woods —
black smoke by the briar.

What do you burn at dusk, my child?
What do you burn in your fire?

Is it the bones of your good man true?
Is it a deed so dire?
Why do the embers burn bright and long?
Why do the flames rise higher?

We have not seen him for many a day,
not since the year it was turning.
Why do you gather the blossoms of May?
And what is it you're burning?

It is not the bones of my good man true.
It is not a deed so dire.
It's the memory of him that burns so long,
that's why the flames rise higher.

I gather up the blossoms of May
to remember the first day we kissed.
He plaited daisies about my neck
and slipped his arm around my waist.

But now he is for a soldier gone
to fight in battles lost and won —
that's why each night I burn this fire,
to light his long journey home.

That's why I stand out here at dusk.
That's why I burn my fire.

Black smoke by the back woods —
black smoke by the briar.

The Girl in the Woods

The girl in the woods could not speak,
    though she knew the sound of words
and could copy their rise and fall,
    but their meaning was not hers.

She sat among the bluebells,
    lost in the chorus of birds
singing sweeter through the trees
    than any voice she had heard.

When they took her to work in the village,
    she smiled as if in a trance —
until at the harvest supper
    she led them all in the dance.

The young men vied to partner her
    and steal a cunning kiss —
and when one stopped to speak with her,
    she followed the twist of his lips.

But the words he spoke span tumbling
    as leaves tossed in a storm,
and though he led her to his house,
    she would not pass through the door.

She walked away then to the wood
     to wait for the whisper of dawn —
and lie among the bluebells there,
     wrapped in the birds' sweet song.

Molly Mawkaby

The river is wide, I cannot get over,
over to the other side —
but there lives Molly Mawkaby
who I mean to be my bride.

'The river is deep, he will never find me,
though he leap and swim in vain.
The river is deep, but it will save me
from ever seeing him again.'

I knew that I would always want her,
swore that she would be my wife —
but now I'm deep in drowning water,
for I need her more than life.

'I know he is a feckless chancer,
roaming round from fair to fair.
He'll never lead me to the altar —
for certain I won't meet him there.'

The river is wide and flowing faster
and I won't make the other side.
Tell sweet Molly if you find her —
it is for her that I have died.

'He had no need to cross the river —
he was a fool to take that risk.
The sky grew dark at our first meeting
one fleeting glance has led to this.

Do not tell me of the currents.
Do not ask me if I cried.
Do not tell me how they found him —
I only know, the river is wide.'

There was a Man

There was a man standing in the wood.

He stood for hours.

He stood for days.

Almost as if he was a tree himself.

And his clothes turned rusty grey,
the colour of old branches
and his skin a furze of green
as the moss spread all about him.

And he stood.

And he waited.

And he saw the birds come and go,
trailing the wind in their tails.

And the insects crawling
through the labyrinth of leaves.

And smelt the wild joy of the sky
singing high above him.

And his boots they took root
as he stood.

And he knew he could never go home.

Oh, the Moon

There in a bone-dry ditch she lies —
    Oh the moon, Oh the moon;
Gazing at the wakening skies —
    Oh the moon, the moon.

For the moon is slow and tardy
    but the night it broke too soon.
She roamed through fields of barley
    to where the lark had flown.

She scrambles out among the briars —
    Oh the moon, the moon;
Her fingers numb, her eyes afire —
    Oh the moon, the moon.

Thorns claw deep inside her
    as she roams the winding wood.
Nettles cannot bind her
    as she greets the moon's slow flood.

She sits in a field of daisies
    out in the morning sun
And picks their petals one by one —
    Oh the moon, the moon has come.

A Moon and a Day

She laid a trail of comfrey seeds
to see who would come that way.
She waited there in the empty house,
she waited a moon and a day.

But all that came were dunocks and crows
who picked away at the seeds —
and no-one could see the path to her house
which wound between the trees.

She laid a trail of ribbons green
to see who would come that way.
She waited there in the orchard,
she waited a moon and a day.

But all that came were bright-eyed girls
who stole the ribbons green —
and no-one could find her orchard there
hidden between the trees.

She laid a trail of glistening tears
to see who would come that way.
She waited there by the garden gate,
she waited a moon and a day.

But all that came were jackdaws bold
for the tears like glittering stones,
as she waited there by the twining rose,
though she waited there alone.

She went out roaming in the woods
to see who she could find.
She wanted to meet a good man there
who was gentle and honest and kind.

But all she found were the tall trees
and the sound of the running stream,
so she went back to her house alone
and wrapped herself in her dreams.

Her dreams were long and weary
and she slept for a moon and a day,
but she awoke to a good man's kiss
as there in his arms she lay.

A Ball of Clay

In his hands a ball of clay
to shape the creatures of the day.

Between her fingers strands of light
to weave the pathways of the night.

They meet at dusk, they meet at dawn
beside dull ditch and twisted thorn.

They speak one word and then move on
to take their journey with the sun
or catch the tresses of the moon
and share again their silent song.

The Darkening Wood

Young William roamed the darkening wood,
All alone and alone,
Where a stone white cottage stood
Lit by the gleam of the moon.

He knocked twice upon the door,
All alone and alone.
Out stepped a woman he did not know,
Dressed in an ash grey gown.

She took him up to her bedroom,
All alone and alone,
And kissed him soft and kissed him long
As through the window the white moon shone.

Her kisses they were a sleeping draught,
All alone and alone,
As they rolled and tumbled, cried and laughed,
Lit by the gleam of the moon.

He dreamt they lay in a green meadow,
All alone and alone.
Her lips were glistening wet with dew
As a far-off blackbird sang.

She bent a branch full ripe with sap,
All alone and alone,
As she cradled him all in her lap
In the folds of her ash grey gown.

Then thunder murmured long and low,
All alone and alone,
Darker than a midnight crow
As she stroked young William's throat.

She wakened then in the misty dawn,
All alone and alone,
To find that William he was gone
By the dying of the moon.

She wailed loud and she wailed long,
All alone and alone,
For all the sorrow she had spun
And the taste of his kisses still on her tongue.

And she was in her room again,
All alone and alone,
Calling William by his name
As she wept in her ash grey gown.

But still she could not know his touch,
All alone and alone,
Though she felt his breath so warm and close
There in the cold grey room.

Now she sings by her open window,
All alone and alone,
Sings to the boy she dreamt in the meadow
To draw him back to her room.

He comes to her by the dark moon's light,
All alone and alone,
And lies with her through the whispering night
There in her empty room.

Now she is not alone in her bed,
Never no more alone,
For wound in her sheets by her pillow-head
Lie young William's pale white bones.

Mary

Mary Joyce: John Clare's childhood sweetheart

She wakes inside the breathing house,
its walls and rafters slowly creaking.

Outside on the scratch of earth,
blood red petals crawl towards the door.

*

In the street she walks with the tall people now
through the bright sunshine,
their lost songs clamouring inside her head,
before she buries their voices
where the bindweed grows —
her fingers scrabbling the loam dark soil.

*

Beneath a dusk of trees a writhing slowness hangs.
No paths lead to the house in the woods:
its walls face every way.

Inside she plays with the skulls of stoats;
a scatter of bones patterns the table.

Beyond dry bracken,
white branches claw through stagnant water.

*

She wanders goose meadows,
the flat lands where no-one comes –
and stands, arms raised,
her neck outstretched
while the dull grey sky squats waiting.

*

In the woods she reaches for herself –
the orb of sun clasped in her hands
high above her head.

She bends to touch speedwell and silverweed,
which lift her up to fly the paths
that wander muddied
through sullen fields of absent cattle.

*

Down brackish lanes she trips and sways,
singing with the shadows
lightly as a moth —

as her fingers run damply
through the furrows of dark fields.

*

She holds a dog rose in her hand
and touches the heart of its throbbing pulse.

In her head the orbs of sun and moon
roll through thunder, wind and rain,
till sweet eclipse sets silence creeping
into the meadow where the stream flows red
and dead fish float, their dull eyes staring.

*

In this night which does not sleep,
in this day that cannot wake,
she counts the planets which turn her blood —
which drag her this way, then this and this,
and gives each one a flower's name
which she can pick, out in the fields
and chain together to make a charm
flung loose about her neck,
as she runs faster than she can think,
thinking quicker than she can trip —
first this way, then this and this,
until she lies beside the ditch
to watch the veil of mottled cloud
which drifts and sways between her fingers
while the planets turn and turn again.

*

She sits huddled as a pigeon under the bridge.
All around a soft mist falls
and the edges of leaves melt into shadow.

The white flowers which glowed so bright last night
are muted now
as their petals taste the rain;

but beneath their roots the stars wait silent
and she can feel them again,
as her fingers begin to burrow and grub.

Slow the Dark Wind Blows

In the field a lone boy stands,
a knot of thunder in each hand.

> *The cart comes rattling slowly.*
> *Slow the bone cart comes.*

Cold lightning clenched behind his eyes,
as in his head the wild geese fly.

> *The grey horse hobbles slowly.*
> *Slow the old horse groans.*

The sky cracks wide, a dance of fire.
His feet root deep into the mire.

> *The hanging air sways slowly.*
> *Slow as silent stones.*

Lost voices twist his bitter tongue
and will not heed the distant drum.

> *The dry dust rises slowly,*
> *and slow the dark wind blows.*

The Waiting Night

This mist in my hands is not mist.
These lips close to mine have not kissed.

These crows in the field squat and speak
with berries red as blood clutched in their beaks.

This path through the woods is strewn with bread.
These creatures that crawl to take it, all are dead.

Where is it you lead me?
What is this hunger that you feed me? –

for the trees are hung with fading light
and the soil tastes dark as waiting night,

and the mist that I hold, so cold to feel
and the wound of your lips will never heal —

no, the wound of your lips will never heal.

Sticks and Clay

I made myself from sticks and clay,
all on a cloudy winter's day.

Two berries plucked to prick my eyes
and gaze upon the leaden skies.

Grey feathers snatched for matted hair
and tattered leaves is all I wear.

Where I go, you cannot tell,
through ditches deep and flooded dell.

When I knock upon your door
and stand outside as winds blow raw,
you cannot see me standing there
to beg for comfort, warmth and cheer.
You do not take me to your hearth,
you do not reckon of my worth –
but as I stumble into night,
I leave for you one candle bright.

Guard it well and watch it burn –
and wait the day when I return.

Leechcraft

'In order to become well,' she said,
'first you must be ill.'

But he lay so quiet,
waiting for the sickness to come,
while outside small birds sang
and a quiet wind rustled the leaves.

'I cannot wait,' he said,
'make me ache again
so that I can be cured.'

She rose from her chair
and pressed her mouth to his brow.

She stroked his limbs gently,
his fingers and then his body
until he was clothed in a dream of sweat.

'There,' she said, as she drew back the curtains
to reveal a crescent moon in a smoke blue sky.

'Soon the fever will begin.'

Orange

Between her fingers
she turned an orange.

'See,' she said, 'it is like
a world. First in shadow,
then in sun.'

He watched as she
peeled the world, dropped
the rind beside her.

'Now the world is naked,'
she said, and placed
her teeth up to its skin.

Her parted lips drank in
the juice. He watched then
as she spat the pips
and sucked upon
the flesh of fruit.

'Now the world is gone,'
she said, her fingers
sticky with it still.

He kissed her long and tasted
the light of world, so sharp
and then the bitter dark.

Now Sing

'Now sing,' she said
but words had dried
in his mouth to a shriveled nut
and spilt dust across
the table where they sat.

Sun slanted through
a high window
and outside they heard
the cry of a fox.

'Why can you not sing?'
she asked
but he shook his head
and placed one hand on hers.

They sat in silence a moment,
listening to the insects
rattling in the wainscot.

At last he cleared his throat.

'I am always singing,'
he whispered.
'Why can you not hear me?'

Her Name

It is an old book which she opens.

The pages are frail.
They have not seen light for many years.

Inside, a name is written.
It is her name, she knows.

But not the name she is known by.
That name has not been spoken
since she came to this place
to live with the dust and the shadows.

She runs one finger over the letters.
Speaks the name out loud.

Soon as she does, the door opens.
A young girl stands there,
wearing a shawl which she once wore,
the key to the door dangling from one finger.

'I heard my name,' says the girl.
'Did you call?'

The Stone

He let the stone sink.

But it returned.
Another day to find it in his pocket,
warm and hard.

And then
in his lover's mouth, cold but
soft.

Then one night, the moon
watching, a frozen
eye.

He threw it again,
this time deep into
the shadows under a tree.

But again, it returned
as bright white berries clinging
to the branches.

He ate them all.
In his fever he heard
them rattle pale as hailstones.

But when he woke,
he opened his fist and
the stone still nestled
in his palm.

The Burning Moon

She held the burning moon in her hands.
Raised it to her face.
Her lips were singed and scorched
as she drank.

Her voice changed then,
a clawing whisper.
And her eyes, her eyes
saw a world inside –
deep and drowning.

Then she sang.
A song of nettles and the pond's deep.
A song of thrushes and a broken stile.

She walked a path
she had never walked before
and came slowly to a door
which opened silent as a sigh.

And there she saw a table
set out with bowl and spoon.

In the bowl a pool of summer's mist
with which she bathed her eyes

till she could see the flowers of dust
that blossomed out across the floor.

Paraselene

He found the moon in the woods.
It had fallen to roll beneath the bushes
and lay there, trapped in a nettle bed.

He spoke to the moon.
The moon listened.
He told how he pitched from his horse.
How he had lain in a ditch
with no way to get home,

how he had eaten red berries that tasted sweet,
taken water from the pond that was sour.

Still the moon listened.

He told how his horse was gone.
He asked the moon
if the horse might make its way home
so that his bride would know
he had fallen and come to find him.

The moon said nothing.

He said to himself –
'My bride won't come to find me.
She will be pleased not to see me again.'

Still the moon said nothing.
and he walked away,
to let the moon rot in the nettle bed.

That night as he slept in another ditch,
he looked up at the stars.
And there he saw the moon.

But not the moon that he met in the woods.

The Pitcher

Each morning she fills a pitcher with water
from the rusty tap in the yard.

She places it on a table beside her bed,
then sets out to work in the fields.

Each evening she returns, weary and thirsty,
to find the pitcher is empty.

Sometimes she wonders who drank it.
Sometimes she does not think about it at all.

Sometimes she wonders
        whose are the dusty footprints
that lead from the yard up the stairs to her room.

Sometimes she wonders who has rumpled the sheets,
who has slept all day in her bed.

One morning she does not fill the pitcher,
but hurries out to the fields.

She cannot remember whether this was deliberate,
or whether she simply forgot.

As she returns at sunset, there are no dusty footprints.
The bed is just as she left it.

But the empty pitcher, dull ochre and brown,
lies smashed in pieces on the floor.

The Memory of Rain

In the darkened room
they slit her stomach open
and took out the key.

They stitched her belly
and left her there,
listening to the wind outside
and the memory of rain.

The key lay beside her
and she stroked it with her fingers,
twisted it slowly,
then placed it on her tongue.

And then she swallowed.

The sweet pleasure
to have it locked inside her
where no-one could see it.

She waited till the darkness faded,
walked through the open door,
trod step by step silently
down the spiraling stairs.

Phantasm

Oh, he is there and I do not know him
but he comes to me in the rain.

Oh, he is pale with dirt on his nails
as he follows me on down the lane.

His hand touches mine
and how swiftly we twine
as our breath mingles quickly together.

As we tumble and play
the rain fades away
and my limbs they are left all a-quiver.

Nobody sees him, nobody knows
how I call for him in the rain,
but my voice it falls dumb
with no words on my tongue
for he never tells me his name.

Seriol's Well

He has fallen here –
to a circle of whitened stone,
the seep of a hidden spring.

The clouds still cling to his shoulders,
a gauze of cobwebs, cold and pale.

Behind the hill, he hears rough singing,
men herded shoulder-to-shoulder,
breathing hard as cattle in a muddied byre.

Above, a choir of birds lifts voices to the wind
as he sits on a lichen rock clutching at torn feathers,
eyes burning candle-bright, alone.

Bidston Hill

Beyond the sky, there is sky.
Beyond water, there is water.

Atop the hill, there is fire.
Inside the fire, there is laughter.

The laughter leads on, along
a path of shadows,

where purple flowers sing
of riven rocks and risen wind,

of a ship that sailed here,
once – to visit scalling rooks,

to glean and carve out names
that were never names before;

and a woman whose eyes
burn wild as the sun,

to lie hidden in the bracken
and then ride on.

The Snowflakes

A mother holds her child in the garden
to watch the snowflakes fall.

His eyes are hardly open
and his clinging fingers small.

She sings to him of summers gone
when she walked slowly in the sun
to watch the sparkling waters run
and turn back home when day was done.

But his eyes are hardly open
and his clinging fingers weak

as she holds him still in the garden,
so cold she cannot speak

of all the roads he has to walk
and all the mountains tall,

as she closes over his clouded eyes —
and still the snowflakes fall.

In the Dust Yard

At dusk, he wrestled with the boy,
hair lank and matted, noses cut and bloodied,
they bore each other down
until they rose, arm in arm
as crows clattered back
to far-off woods when darkness came.

Then trudged the long path
across the bridge, beyond the sawpits,
each to the coldness of his own waiting door.

Now they sit, long years later,
eyes clouded over, dust clinging to their jackets,
pint glasses almost empty,
as they wait another round.

Elven Boy

He did not seem an elven boy,
just some lad like any other.

He stood alone at the edge of the fair,
but then would go no further.

She said she'd meet him for a dare,
where the other girls could watch and stare.

Her fingers combed his ragged hair –
his shirt was torn, his arms were bare,

but he did not seem an elven boy,
just some lad like any other.

She placed one arm around his waist
and brushed the down upon his face.

She led him from the fair's bright lights
into the dark of the waiting night.

She kissed him once, but he turned away
and as she begged him twice to stay,

he smiled as he took her arm
and said they could not come to harm

but when the others searched next day,
both the girl and the lad were gone.

Feral

We have our own tongue
and will not come
to any name you call us.

Ours are the shadow-ways,
the prowl and yowl
you do not see –
you only hear
but never understand.

Ours are the eyes
of night, the ghost walk
on along brick walls,
the skulk and scowl
to root out secrets
your nose cannot even smell.

How can you tell
what it is we dream
through day-long sleep
when we just seem
to be breathing slow
and waiting for a dark
that you always turn
and hide from.

Jenny-Many-Names

They called her 'lack-wit', called her 'frit',
they called her Jenny-Many-Names.

She watched them chasing on the green
but would not join their many games.

When thunder rolled and storm clouds broke,
she stood out laughing in the rain.

When black smoke choked as hay-ricks blazed,
they said was Jenny lit the flames.

When milk turned sour and rats stole flour,
they chased her out down miry lanes.

But she came back, again, again,
bearing flowers of many names.

She brought back comfrey, brought back rue;
she boiled up ragwort in a stew.

Now who do they visit when their babes get sick,
when they need a potion quick as quick,
to cure their fever, ease their pain? –

They seek out Jenny-Many-Names.

Barbara Ann

Where are the stars tonight, Barbara Ann?
Where is the wanting moon?
What is that stone that you wear at your neck
and why have you lain here so long?

Where is the westering wind, Barbara Ann,
that blew through the folds of your cloak?
What is that potion that clings to your tongue
and seeps sweet as breath down your throat?

What is that look in your eyes, Barbara Ann,
as if you see more than you tell?
What are the seeds that you sowed in the field
and what was cast into the well?

Come to me now, Barbara Ann —
ride the grey horse to the dawn,
through meadows and streams,
through shadows and dreams,
till the veil of silence is torn.

Smoke Road

He took the old smoke road
down to the coast,
down where the snake wind crawls;
down where tattoos of silence
wash empty along the shore.

He took the old smoke road
back to the hills,
back where the hard fire lures;
back where the track near crumbles away
in the mist as the ghost eagle calls.

He left the old smoke road
deep in the night,
dark behind unbolted doors;
deep in the sound of loss turned around,
laid in a cradle of thorns.

Silences Still to be Heard

The wind slipped softly into the ditch
where she felt a trickle of water
tickle at her lips.

What did the water say? What did it whisper?

It whispered of winters creeping towards them.
It whispered of silences still to be heard.

It whispered of other winds that no-one had seen yet,
speaking in voices that no-one would know.

*

The tree held the rain in her arms.

The rain had been journeying and returned.

A journey of clouds and rivers and marshland.
A journey of mist and ice and flood.

But now the tree held her.
She breathed again.
A journey of sap and moss and root.

*

The wind bore a feather.

Bore it from bramble to blossom to tree,
but no-one knew which bird had lost it.

Some said a dove, a sparrow, a hawk.
One said an eagle, a heron, a crow.

But none of them knew.

And the dull dust said
was the feather of the grey bird
which came once at dawn
to sing that mountains had fallen
and deserts lay frozen.
But none remembered the song.

*

The river slept.

She dreamt of fish that swam
brighter than the stars which drowned in her belly.

She dreamt of pebbles
which whispered secrets older than the wind.

She dreamt of the creature
that came once
and peered deep into the mirror of her eyes.

But the river slept on
and dreamt of fox calls darker than night
and reeds which stretched tall towards the sun.

The river slept on
and forgot the creature.
And the creature never came again.

*

The eagle saw it all.
From the top of the mountain, the eagle saw it all.

And what he saw, he told the wind
which raced through skies and over oceans.
And the wind knew all that the eagle saw.

So she whispered to the thunder,
who roared and ripped and rolled
with all that the eagle saw.

All that the eagle saw
flashed in the eyes of the lightning
to burn out the tree's blighted craw.

The tree cracked and toppled
but, trapped inside every leaf,
was all that the eagle saw.

The mouse found one leaf and she hid in its shadow,
and though she was very small,
there safe inside the green of the leaf
she saw all that the eagle saw.

*

There were clouds in the sky,

but the rain did not fall.
The leaf heard a sigh
but it wasn't the wind.

Dust touched the petals
as they hung frail and dry.

The stone slept on
in the heat of the sun.

*

The ice shivered.
She had never thawed,
but when she melted a new rain came.

The new rain brought a season
that the birds had never seen.

The dust was slaked.
The rivers spilled.

This was a season of changing light,
of burning moons, of sleepless dreams.

In the ditch, a lizard woke
and crawled towards the rain.

*

The sparrow woke.

She knew that she was hungry
and filled her belly with berries,
but the berries tasted bitter.

She drank water from a puddle,
but the puddle was sick with smoke.

She flapped her wings then
to perch in the branches of a tree

and the tree rocked her gently
while the spiders spun their threads
till she was wrapped in a web
safe from the silence and the rain.

*

Nothing grew there now.

It was a place where the winds came,
and the wintering.

A place where the stones lay,
and the grass seeded memories of tall trees
and the hawks which hovered overhead.

They looked to the clouds
and felt the pulse of the wind.

They looked deep into each other's eyes
till one led the way
and the others followed slowly.

*

There was a storm which came.

The grass spoke of it, the leaves and the blossom.

None knew where it came from.
It did not fly with the clouds.
It did not fall from the sky.
It did not swim in the river's deep water.

But it came, they said.

And knew that it would come again.

*

The sparrow spoke to the sky.
The sky murmured back
in the cold dawn of morning.

The sparrow hacked out a complaint.
The sky smiled and stretched,
dreaming of the sun.

The sparrow argued and raged.
The sky shrugged and muttered dull thunder.

The sparrow shook his feathers
in the dry hungry dust.
The sky laughed and sent down the rain.

*

A new thunder came then,
a thunder they had never heard before.

There had been no lightning in the darkness
and none of them felt rain,
but the new thunder came.

The blackbird trilled with the pleasure of it,
but the sparrow trembled in fear.
The robin stood, and his bright eyes glared,
but the new thunder came.

It rode through the hills
and the river waters shivered.
All across the meadows, the long grasses quivered.

*

They found a skull by the dry river bed.
Its eyes stared empty.
As they sniffed the air for the searing wind,
they could not tell what creature it had been
or what it had dreamed.

They could not tell how long it had lain in the sun.
Even its bones had gone.

*

Oh to sing, but they could not sing.
They could not walk or crawl or fly.

They could only watch,
though their eyes were closed.

The sun had not risen,
though it was day.

They could only taste the silence
hanging heavy in the sky.

*

In the heat of the sun, they slept.

As they slept, they dreamt they were curled
inside an egg.

Beyond its shell they could hear
voices they had never heard before.

When they woke, it was cold.
They shivered, still curled,
listened, but heard nothing.

They curled closer and slept again.
From the distance came a soft, plaintive cry.

*

A hunger was in the land.

It gnawed at the soil, the rocks and the stones.
It drank from the clouds, the rivers and streams.

It devoured the flowers, the trees and the scrub.

The birds flew from it,
the horses, the lions.

They cowered from the hunger in shadows and
caves.

But the hunger stalked by them
as it consumed its own greed,
its bile and its poison.

A hunger was in the land.
The creatures watched in silence
as the hunger ate itself.

*

The yellow flower stretched tendon and sinew,

till white seed sprang, took to the wind
and floated far across the river
to nestle in the moist damp soil.

There another flower grew,
but she choked on the dust which drifted down
as thunder muttered deep in the ground.

*

In the morning they heard a voice.

It was not the voice of the flowers singing.
It was not the voice of the rain laughing.
It was not the voice of the birds complaining.

It came from over the mountain.
It told of a river they had never seen.

One of them spoke to ask what voice it was –
and when the answer came,
they knew it was their own.

*

The breath was new.

It had not breathed before,
had never entered a mouth,
touched teeth, travelled
across a tongue into the labyrinth of lungs.

The breath was clean.

It had not tasted pollen,
smelt smoke or swallowed dust.

It had not washed in the cold grey rain.
It had not coughed up dirt.

*

The crows clustered at the river's edge
on the flat mud where the gulls sat.

They rode the rhythm of the water,
the rhythm of the wind,
as their voices hung in the grey light
heavy with rumours of oceans.

But their heads turned again
to stare darkly back to the marshlands
and the dull bitter mulch of the soil.

*

A thirst of thunder and the ache of rain.

The dark stones lay in the dry land
as the dust danced,
as the grey light sang,
as the dull wind muttered

and beyond the slow stalking hunger,
the bones of the mountain stirred.

*

Out of the thigh of thunder
sprang lightning.

She danced in the meadows,
she scorched the white flowers.

Their petals were gathered
in the arms of the blizzard.

Claw and talon and the bloodied thorn.

*

A shadow whispered in the mist.
It spoke without a voice.

It touched without feather, fur or claw.
It moved without limb or wing.

It flew, it crawled.

Its eyes were berry bright,
but it saw nothing at all.

*

Ravens stripped away the flesh.
Wind pecked at the bones.
Beetles crawled where eyes had been
to see the journeys which had gone,
the forest where the dark smoke rose,
the restless rolling of the sun.

*

A purple flower crawled from the pilth.
Dark birds tore at the mulch and slime.

Marshes seeped where the ice had been.
Rivers bled through rotting mud.
A gaunt wind rode the flatlands.

*

What came from stone?
A whisper.

What came from whisper?
A flood.

What came from flood?
A breathing.

What came from breath?
A flower.

What came from flower?
A dark wing.

What came from dark wing?
The thunder.

What came from thunder?
A stone.

*

The seed of the blood was planted
deep into the ache of the ground.

The warm night coiled her body close,
nurturing its hunger.

A thin wind beat its wings and waited
as the red seed stretched and burst
and the blood walked on shaking legs
across the hard flat earth.

*

In a nest of knotted thunder
lay eggs of bitter rain.

They hatched in darkness.
A storm bird crawled,
its throat raw with smoke.

It stumbled crabbed and silent,
opened wide its bone white beak
and swallowed down the moon.

*

The paths were already there –
they just had to find them.

Path to the blood-red stream.
Path to the silent mountain.

The paths away from whispering dreams,
the rotted stump, the broken chant,
forgotten faces dancing.

Until they came to a forest
where there were no paths,
where uncertain shadows waited –
as fallen branches forced them back
to look up to the sky and onward.

*

They came to this place
to make offerings:

a grain of salt,
a stone sucked dry.

They placed them where the shadows met,
covered them with a fist of dust,

spoke words they found in a dead bird's nest
and then walked on, towards the sun.

*

In his hands he held two knots of smoke.
In his eyes, the fire.

Behind him the shadows still danced
as he walked away from the silence

towards the beating of drums.
Towards the drowning of rivers.
Towards the whispering tongues.

He knew, beyond the mountain
would be hunger –
and there at last he could feed.

*

They hung his body in the bones of the tree
and left him there to sing.

He sang of seasons of darkness,
of a river which drank its own tears.

He sang of the moon in a silent field,
but when a grey bird came to peck
at his eyes
she found they were already taken,
that two white stones were waiting there –
watching for the storm.

The Blunted Axe

From the hack of the tree, raw sap flows.
It seeps as slow as tears, as woes

that he kept trapped deep in his blood,
of moments lost and words unsaid

that tumble out, though none will hear,
for in this wood no-one comes near.

But in his mind he sets a fire,
a cottage lit, the smouldering thatch,
timbers falling as they crack.

As it burns, he turns his back
and swings again the blunted axe.

Acknowledgements

With thanks to Eleanor Rees for editorial advice, insight, support and inspiration.

Some of these poems appeared in
The Blunted Axe (Dreich Chapbook #6);
Masculinity anthology (Broken Sleep Books);
Earth Pathways Diary 2023;
and in the magazines *Abridged, Black Nore Review, The Crank, Duck's Head Journal, Eunoia Review, Grimoire Silvanus, Ink Pantry* and *Moof.*

DAVID WARD was born in Northampton. He is co-founder of The Windows Project, running creative writing workshops in community venues on Merseyside since 1976; and editor of *Smoke* magazine. He has toured to Singapore, where he was visiting Writer-in-Residence Nanyang University; Hong Kong and Harbin (Northern China). Broadcast on BBC TV and radio. Poems in over 200 magazines and anthologies.

Collections:
Jambo (Riot Stories Ltd and Impact 1993)
Tracts (Headland 1996)
On the Edge of Rain (Headland 2009)
Inside Pale Eyes (Hawkwood 2019)

For children:
Candy and Jazzz (Oxford University Press 1994)
The Tree of Dreams (Collins 1996)

Writing as David Greygoose:
folkloric tales
Brunt Boggart (Hawkwood 2015; Pushkin 2018),
Mandrake Petals and Scattered Feathers
(Hawkwood 2021),
Crow Dark Dawn (Hawkwood 2023).